Bill Gates
Computer Legend

Sara Barton-Wood

RAINTREE
STECK-VAUGHN
PUBLISHERS

A Harcourt Company

Austin   New York
www.raintreesteckvaughn.com

Titles in this series:
Muhammad Ali: The Greatest
Neil Armstrong: The First Man on the Moon
Fidel Castro: Leader of Cuba's Revolution
Diana: The People's Princess
Anne Frank: Voice of Hope
Bill Gates: Computer Legend
Martin Luther King, Jr: Civil Rights Hero
Nelson Mandela: Father of Freedom
Mother Teresa: Saint of the Slums
Pope John Paul II: Pope for the People
Queen Elizabeth II: Monarch of Our Times
The Queen Mother: Grandmother of a Nation

Published by Raintree Steck-Vaughn Publishers, an imprint of Steck-Vaughn Company

Library of Congress Cataloging-in-Publication Data

Wood, Sara, 1952-
  Bill Gates, computer giant / Sara Barton-Wood.
    p. cm. -- (Famous lives)
  Includes bibliographical references and index.
  ISBN 0-7398-4432-6
  1. Gates, Bill, 1955- 2. Businessmen--United States--
Biography--Juvenile literature. [1. Gates, Bill, 1955- 2.
Businesspeople. 3. Microsoft Corporation--History.]
  I. Title II. Famous lives (Austin, Tex.)

HC102.5.G38 W66 2001
338.7'610053'092--dc21
[B]
                                                    2001019514

Printed in Italy. Bound in the United States.

1 2 3 4 5 6 7 8 9 0 LB 06 05 04 03 02

Picture Acknowledgments
The publisher would like to thank the following for their kind permission to use these pictures: Associated Press (title page), 5, 13, 32, 37, 39 (top), 43, 44; Corbis (cover), 10, 11, 15, 20, 21, 23, 24, 27, 28, 30/ Sygma © G. Haller, Seattle Post Intelligencer 33/ © Darryl Heikes 39 (bottom); Robert Harding 14; Lakeside School 8, 9, 12; Microsoft 17, 19, 22, 26, 29; Robert Opie 16 (top and bottom); Photri 7, 25, 31; Pictorial 6; Popperfoto 4, 34, 35, 36, 38, 40, 41, 42, 45 (top and bottom); Topham Picturepoint 18.

Contents

Launchpad

It is August 24, 1995. In fifteen marquees on a lawn outside an office in Redmond, Seattle, 2,500 guests are drinking champagne. The air is filled with the buzz of excited voices as the guests watch a revolutionary new computer program. This is the launch of Windows 95.

A roar goes up as Bill Gates, President of Microsoft, the company that developed Windows, arrives. He and talk-show host Jay Leno take the stage. They swap jokes about the new technology. Gates claims it will change the way people communicate with each other in the 21st century —and beyond.

Bill Gates (left) and Jay Leno entertain the world's press at the launch of Windows 95.

A silhouette of Gates on the stage at the Windows' launch.

Gates was right. Sales of the new program soared well over 30 million in its first year. Windows became a household name. The program put "a computer on every desk and in every home" as Gates had predicted in 1975. This is the story of a teenager who turned his fascination with computers into a multi-million dollar business and became one of the wealthiest people in the world. Later he gave a large amount of his fortune away to charity.

> *"People don't want to settle for outdated features or performance. A three-year-old computer is about as popular as a three-year-old newspaper."*
> Bill Gates, *The Road Ahead*, 1995.

Early Life

Star Trek! *This is how people in the 1960s thought the future might look. We are not able to travel in space like the television characters, but computers certainly play a large part in our lives.*

Unlike many self-made men, Bill Gates did not have to fight his way up from a poor background. He was born on October 28, 1955 in Seattle, Washington, into a prosperous local business family. His father is a lawyer, his grandfather was a banker. His mother was a teacher before she married and had a family.

Gates was a very strong-willed, active child who liked to rock himself in his cradle and on his toy rocking-horse. Even now, Gates often rocks backward and forward, sometimes violently, in his chair. He says it helps him concentrate. Others say it shows that he is slightly autistic.

Family life has always been important to him. Gates says that he remembers the atmosphere at home with his parents and two sisters as "a rich environment in which to learn." The whole family enjoyed reading, playing board games and cards, especially bridge, and solving puzzles. Winning mattered a great deal! Perhaps this early experience of good-natured competition prepared him for the intensity and seriousness of business life later on.

This is the famous Seattle skyline showing the Space Needle (built for the World Fair in 1962), and Mount Rainier in the background.

School

As a schoolboy, Gates was so clever, especially at math and science, that he did not have to try very hard. The other kids teased him because he was at the top of his class all the time. But his easy success and the taunting stopped him from making friends. So, he started making mistakes on purpose to bring his grades down.

Lakeside School had many rigid rules and discipline and lots of very intelligent students.

In 1967, Bill's parents realized that he was gifted and decided to move him to Lakeside School, a private school with other outstanding pupils. Gates soon found that he did not always earn the "top student" distinction, even when he was trying.

Gates in the school's computer room. In the bottom left-hand corner is a teletype machine which connected to a computer via the telephone.

Although 11-year-old Gates was small and shy, he was already extremely competitive. He loved a fast game of tennis, and the thrill of skiing both on water and on snow. He also went to summer camp with his friends from Lakeside, where he enjoyed the challenge of outdoor adventures. But what he remembers most vividly from his days at Lakeside was the first time he used a computer. He quickly developed a passion for the machine that was to play such a large part in his life later.

"I couldn't imagine how an 11-year-old could have a mind like that. He memorized three chapters of the Bible—and he had a deep understanding of the words as well." Reverend Dale, the church pastor of the University Congregational Church, which the Gates family attended.

Computers Before Gates

Small, personal computers with a screen, keyboard, and printer, like those in school classrooms today, had not been invented yet. What Gates discovered at Lakeside was a teletype machine. This records information by punching holes on a paper tape. The pattern made by the holes was the earliest form of software. The machine was connected via the telephone to a mainframe computer at a local General Electric office.

Computers were so expensive in the late 1960s that only really big companies could afford them. They were also so big that one computer filled a whole room! So smaller companies, and some schools such as Lakeside, "bought" time on a computer wherever one was available.

A woman sits at a large computer board at the Gorodok Academy, Center for Space Studies in the Soviet Union, in 1967.

Nobody at Lakeside, students or teachers, knew how to write the complicated code of holes punched on tape that would tell the computer what to do. But Gates, teaching himself from a handbook, quickly discovered that he could get the computer to solve mathematical puzzles. If he wrote the code correctly, he got a useful answer. If he wrote it wrong, the computer did not understand what was required. It was a challenge he could not resist.

This is how computers looked in the 1950s. Only someone with a real vision of the future, like Gates, could imagine the transformation to today's personal computers.

"The computer I used (at school) was huge and cumbersome and slow and absolutely compelling."
Bill Gates, from his book *The Road Ahead*, 1995.

The Lakeside Programmers

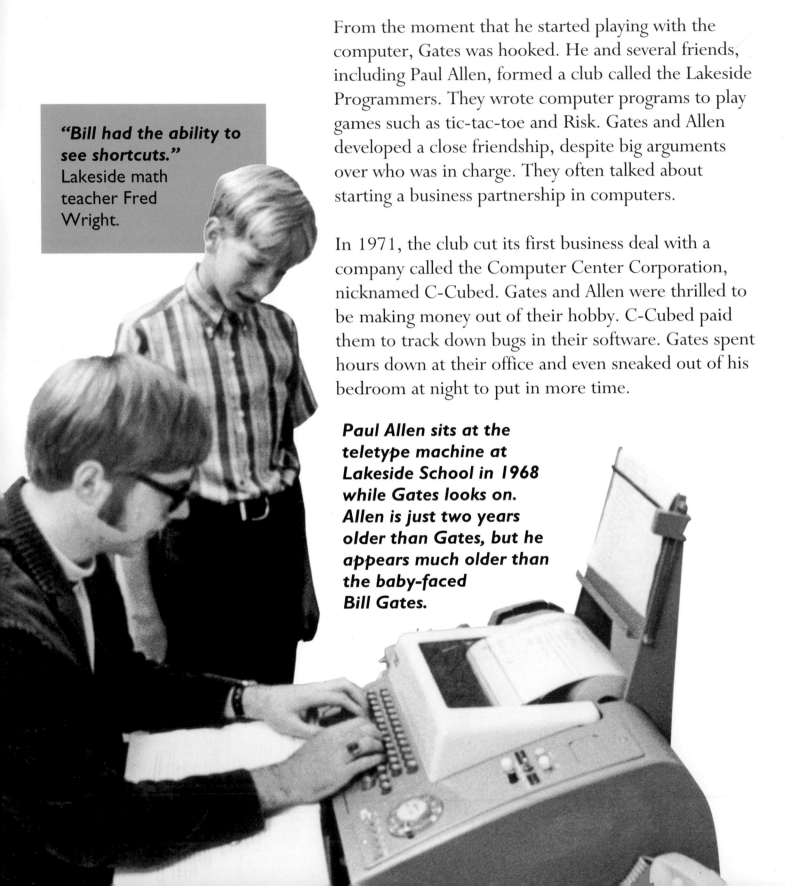

From the moment that he started playing with the computer, Gates was hooked. He and several friends, including Paul Allen, formed a club called the Lakeside Programmers. They wrote computer programs to play games such as tic-tac-toe and Risk. Gates and Allen developed a close friendship, despite big arguments over who was in charge. They often talked about starting a business partnership in computers.

In 1971, the club cut its first business deal with a company called the Computer Center Corporation, nicknamed C-Cubed. Gates and Allen were thrilled to be making money out of their hobby. C-Cubed paid them to track down bugs in their software. Gates spent hours down at their office and even sneaked out of his bedroom at night to put in more time.

Paul Allen sits at the teletype machine at Lakeside School in 1968 while Gates looks on. Allen is just two years older than Gates, but he appears much older than the baby-faced Bill Gates.

This is how children at school today learn to use computers. Gates is eager to give money to schools to buy computers, perhaps because when the children grow up, they will all buy his products!

Another company paid them $5,000 to write a program to work out weekly pay for their employees. They also wrote programs to analyze information about traffic flow for the police. By now, Gates's school days were coming to an end. With top grades in most subjects, he easily was accepted by the top-ranked Harvard University to study math.

Harvard

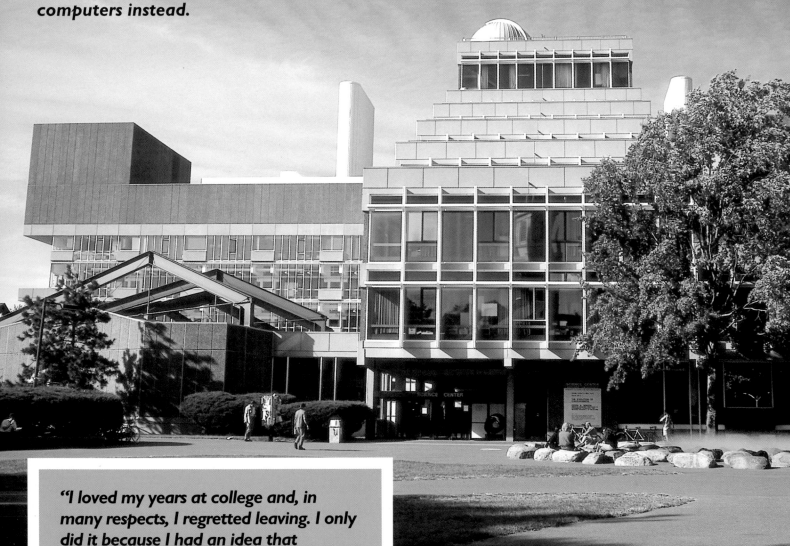

The modern science school at Harvard University in Boston, Massachusetts. Gates was outclassed in mathematics, his chosen subject, so he concentrated on computers instead.

Student life suited Bill Gates, but he lived very irregular hours. Freed from the timetable laid down by home and high school, he sometimes went for days without sleep. Living on a diet of pizza and Coke, he often worked for 36 hours without a break. Then he would sleep under the desk.

"I loved my years at college and, in many respects, I regretted leaving. I only did it because I had an idea that couldn't wait."
Bill Gates, *The New York Times*, May 8, 1996.

Gates spent most of his time in the computer center at Harvard. He worked for weeks on a program for a computer baseball game. This meant using complex mathematical formulas to represent figures hitting, throwing, and catching a baseball. Even when he was asleep, he dreamed about computers. A fellow student remembers hearing him talk in code as he lay on the floor!

He was not at all interested in the social side of university life. Apart from all-night poker sessions or going to a movie, he rarely took time off. Nobody can remember him ever dating a girl at Harvard. But he did make one good friend, Steve Ballmer. Ballmer later joined Microsoft as assistant to the boss.

This is Steve Ballmer speaking at a business conference in 1998. Like Gates, Ballmer can go for days without sleep and is passionate about the computer business.

The Revolution Begins

On a cold winter day in December 1974, during Gates's second year at Harvard, Paul Allen came to visit. As Allen was walking across the college campus, he spotted at a newspaper stand the January issue of *Popular Electronics*. He had read the magazine since he was a schoolboy at Lakeside. On the front cover was a picture of a new computer, the Altair 8800.

Above: **The first typewriter was made in 1874. It didn't need electricity and it was portable. In their own way, early typewriters were revolutionary because people could produce print-like documents at work and home.**

Left: **The electric typewriter was introduced in 1935. It was quicker and more efficient than the earlier typewriters but it was still difficult to correct mistakes.**

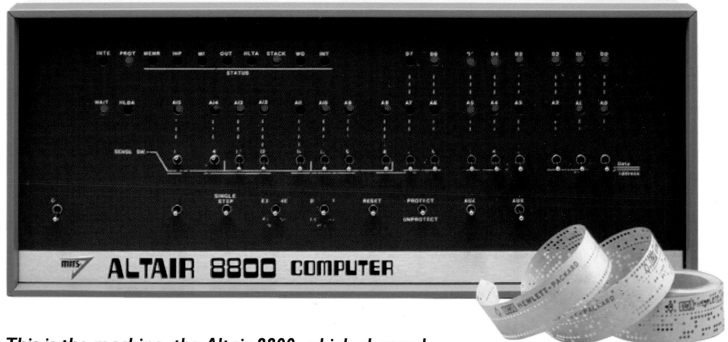

ALTAIR 8800 COMPUTER

This is the machine, the Altair 8800, which changed the course of Gates's life and started the computer revolution. In front is a piece of paper tape punched with holes carrying instructions for the machine.

The magazine was advertising the world's first microcomputer. It was a rectangular, metal machine with switches and lights on the front. The magazine's readers could buy the machine in kit form and build their own computer.

Allen's heart pounded with excitement as he bought a copy of the magazine and read the report. He realized at once that this machine marked the start of the computer revolution. It was the moment he and his friend Bill Gates had been waiting for. He rushed off to find Gates, who was playing poker. Allen dragged him away from the game shouting "Look! Look! It's happening. We've got to do something."

Blazing a Trail

Albuquerque in New Mexico, is a city in the middle of a desert. After work Gates liked to escape to the sand dunes and drive his car at high speed.

The company making the Altair 8800 was called MITS, based in Albuquerque, New Mexico. MITS needed a computer program to make the machine work. Gates and Allen called to say they had a program ready. In fact, they did not. But they felt sure they could write one and they were desperate to get in first. They knew many other people would be trying to do the same.

For the next eight weeks, Gates worked almost non-stop at the Harvard computer center. He was adapting a computer language called BASIC—Beginners' All-purpose Symbolic Instruction Code. Allen, who had a job in Boston, joined him when he could. They were blazing a trail. No one had ever written code for a microcomputer before. Some people said it was not possible.

At the end of eight weeks Allen flew down to Albuquerque with the finished program. They had not even tested it because they could not get hold of an Altair 8800. Allen held his breath as he fed the program into MITS' computer. It worked the very first time.

Bill Gates with Paul Allen. Together, they co-founded Micro-Soft.

Micro-Soft

Ed Roberts, the owner of MITS, was impressed. Not only did he agree to buy their program, he also offered Paul Allen a job as director of software. Allen moved to live in Albuquerque while Gates continued his studies at Harvard.

In April 1975, Gates and Allen formed the business partnership they had talked of at school. They called it Micro-Soft. Though Gates was still only 19, he showed his tough business sense in the deal with Roberts. He refused to sell the program outright. Instead he insisted on a license, or leasing agreement. That gave MITS the exclusive right to sell the software with the Altair 8800. This has now become the standard, or usual, way of doing business in the world of computer software.

Demand was enormous. Paul Allen soon gave up his job with MITS to work full-time for Micro-Soft. Back at Harvard, Gates had to decide. Should he finish his degree or strike out on his own? After much soul-searching, and against the wishes of his parents, he finally decided in favor of his new business. It was a decision he has not regretted.

By the 1980s, the computer revolution was in full swing with the introduction of microcomputers. Worldwide, offices were installing their first computers.

"Life for us was working, and maybe going to a movie, and then working some more. Sometimes we were so tired we would fall asleep in front of customers."
Bill Gates, *The New York Times*, March 14, 1995, talking about life in Albuquerque from 1976–79.

21

Fighting Spirit

The Micro-Soft team (Gates bottom left, Allen bottom right) pose for a photograph. Nearly all of them are just like Gates—young, male, and crazy about computers and software.

Neither Allen nor Gates had much time for Ed Roberts. Gates, in particular, thought Roberts ran his business badly. Roberts, for his part, thought Gates was a spoiled rich kid, who lost his temper when he did not get his own way. This is true—even Gates admits that he shouts and calls people names when things go wrong. Added to this, Gates still looked about 13-years-old and had a high, squeaky voice. He was not taken seriously. There were frequent heated arguments.

The trouble was that Micro-Soft depended on MITS to sell their product. MITS soon stopped trying to sell the product because it was easy to make illegal copies of the software.

Gates realized that to make any real money, Micro-Soft had to break away from MITS. Then he could go after sales himself. There was a big legal battle lasting nine months and Micro-Soft nearly went out of business. In the end Micro-Soft won. Bill Gates breathed a sigh of relief. But it had taught him a valuable lesson about the need to be ruthless.

Gates always looked younger than his age. But as soon as he started talking about computers, people were astounded at his knowledge.

"Most of you steal your software. Hardware must be paid for but software is something to share. Who cares if the people who worked on it get paid?" From Bill Gates's angry letter complaining about piracy published in a computer magazine in 1975.

The Big Break

The orders for software rolled in and Micro-Soft thrived. Sales soon topped $1 million a year. But it was difficult to get good programmers to move to Albuquerque. No one wanted to live out in the desert. So in 1979 Gates and Allen moved the company to Seattle. Their dozen employees moved with them. Micro-Soft lost the hyphen in its name, becoming Microsoft.

By this time the computer industry was "going crazy." It seemed everyone wanted to be part of the new industry. IBM was easily the biggest player in the computer market. So when the company approached Gates in 1980 about a program for their new personal computer, Gates sat up and took notice.

The Microsoft offices in Seattle are spread out over a large area. They are designed to make everyone feel on the same level, from the office cleaner to the company president.

By contrast, the IBM tower in Atlanta, Georgia, is a skyscraper. This older, more established company has many different floors.

To start with, IBM needed an operating system. Gates said he could have one ready within a year. He knew of a system he could buy and adapt. He paid just $75,000 for the system, modified it and called it MS-DOS, standing for Microsoft Disk Operating System. MS-DOS was sold with every IBM computer. But, learning from his previous experience with MITS, Gates retained the right to sell MS-DOS to other companies as well. Before long, Gates was selling MS-DOS to everyone.

The Appliance of Science

But the operating system was only half the story when it came to software. The IBM PC, and all the other computers, also needed an application.

An application turns a computer into a very specialized machine. If you install a word-processing application, you then have a word processor. Another application will turn the computer into a machine that deals with spreadsheets (for working out accounts). A third application might be a game. Gates realized the applications market was worth a great deal of money. He decided to get Microsoft heavily involved. With Bill Gates, there is always a drive to achieve more.

Microsoft employees relax outside the Microsoft office at lunchtime.

Microsoft's Word program for word processors was launched in 1983. It was fast and very powerful. It had a mouse to point and click instead of using complex instructions on a keyboard. It also used color pictures instead of words for some of the choices on the menu. It looked good and, even more important, it was very easy to use. Gates wanted everyone to own a computer. It was part of his vision of the future.

With the right applications, Bill Gates realized that computers could be used by the whole family, as well as by professionals and office workers.

"Bill was furious when Lotus (a Microsoft competitor) came out with a spreadsheet program that was better than ours. He knew that applications was where the money was."
A programmer at Microsoft, 1983.

Computer Wars

The Microsoft executives (left to right) Jon Shirley, Bill Gates, and Steve Ballmer in 1985.

Microsoft was becoming a highly successful company. In 1985, it sold over $140 million worth of products and employed thousands of people. In 1986, the company was floated on the New York Stock Exchange. Gates became a millionaire overnight. The following year he became the world's youngest-ever billionaire.

"The bitterness was unbelievable. People were really upset. Gates was sucking IBM dry."
A former IBM designer quoted in Bill Gates Speaks.

But Microsoft and Gates had made many enemies. Paul Allen, a more laid-back, relaxed man, retired from the business in 1982 because he became ill. This left Gates in sole charge. He was ruthless against competitors, and he could be rude and sarcastic. Some companies refused to do business with Microsoft because their methods were so underhanded. Apple even sued Microsoft in court claiming they stole some of their ideas. But Apple lost.

Perhaps the toughest battle was with IBM. Trust between the two companies broke down. In 1989, the partnership with IBM came to an end. Both sides blamed the other for the split. IBM decided to write its own software. Gates now found himself competing against the biggest computer company in the world, instead of selling to it.

Windows

Would Microsoft make it without IBM? As usual, Gates had an ace up his sleeve and he liked nothing better than a game of poker. Only this time, the stakes were millions of dollars.

The ace up Gates's sleeve was Windows. Gates gambled the whole future of Microsoft on this new system which replaced MS-DOS. Two earlier versions of Windows had already been released. Both failed to sell. But Windows 3.0, which came out in 1990, was a bestseller. It was faster, more powerful, and with much more space to store information. Now the computer could run several applications at the same time, so the user could switch from spreadsheets to a database or to writing a letter on a word processor with one point-and-click of the mouse. It allowed a "window" into the different applications.

*Bill Gates receives a technical excellence award from **PC** Magazine in November 1986.*

Still Gates pushed on. Windows 3.1 came out two years later with many more improvements. It was installed in 70 million personal computers in its first year. And 90 percent of new computers were sold with the new program. IBM's product, OS/2, was completely outclassed by Windows.

"Microsoft is now driving the industry, not IBM."
Fred Gibbons in *The Wall Street Journal*, January 1991.

Gates took an enormous risk when he decided to continue to invest in Windows. This has become now one of the most familiar screen images in the world.

Marriage to Melinda

Just a week after their wedding, the Gates's attended a party in their honor back home in Seattle. Gates is twisting the ring on his wedding finger, getting used to his new status as a married man.

Work always came first for Bill Gates. This left him little time for a social life or dating girls. But no one who knew him well ever doubted that he would one day get married.

Melinda French made a big impression on Gates when she joined Microsoft as a business manager in 1987. Nine years younger than Gates, she was born and grew up in Dallas, Texas. She was also able to cope with Gates's fiery personality!

This photo is of the secret marriage ceremony held on a cliff-top overlooking the Pacific Ocean. Photographers were not supposed to take pictures but some obviously managed.

"When I'm 35, I'll get married." Bill Gates talking about marriage in *The Making of Microsoft* by Daniel Ichbiah and Susan L Knepper. He didn't marry Melinda until he was 38.

According to people who know Melinda she is "funny, intelligent, and very intense." She is also obsessive about privacy. She will not talk to the press and has forbidden family and friends to talk publicly about her private life as well.

She and Gates dated on and off for several years before finally getting engaged in 1993. Gates showed a romantic streak by flying Melinda to Omaha, Nebraska, one Sunday morning. His friend Warren Buffett had Borsheim's, his jewelry store, opened especially for them so they could pick out a ring. They got married in Hawaii in January 1994.

33

The World's Richest Man

Anyone expecting that marriage would slow Bill Gates down was in for a rude shock. His many competitors, and his enemies, were probably hoping that his python-like grip on the software market would ease off. Unhappily for them, the squeeze got tighter.

"This is my life. It's what I am. It's what I get excited about."
Bill Gates talking about his work,
The Sunday Times, November 1999.

The launch of Windows 95 was delayed several times because it was vital to include an Internet browser. In this photo, Gates explains how it works to customers in Seattle.

Windows had already virtually cornered the market when Windows 95 came out. But this latest operating system took computing much further. It was much faster than before. There was enough power to run booking systems for hotels and airlines. It could operate CD-ROMs, the fax machine, e-mail, and the Internet. A technical problem had been corrected so the system did not crash so often. It would change the way people worked, shopped, gossiped, made vacation reservations, and bought theater tickets.

By the end of 1995, Gates was said to be the world's wealthiest man. He owned $12.9 billion of Microsoft shares without even counting his annual income. He had done all this without borrowing one cent from his parents.

Getting ready for lift-off! A Microsoft employee opens the Windows 95 program just before the release of the new software.

35

The Lakeside Home

It looks more like a building site than a home but the interior of the Lakeside house was completed when this photo was taken in September 1997.

So what kind of home would the world's richest man like to live in? To start with, it had to be big. It also had to be very private with lots of security. And, being a man with a vision of the future, Gates made sure everything was controlled by state-of-the-art computer technology.

The house has 45 rooms in seven main pavilions linked by underground passageways. It stands on the shore of beautiful Lake Washington, surrounded by five acres of pleasant woodland. No one can get into the property without passing guards at the gate. It cost about $50 million and took seven years to build. Gates once said it felt as though he had been building a house all his life.

The property's "brain" is a central computer room. This controls everything—the video-art walls, the doors that open and close, and the lights that go on and off automatically. It also controls the music that follows you around the house, the temperature of the water in your bath, and even the climate in the rest of the house! Just in case the computer crashes, there are manual on-off switches as well.

"I wanted technology to play a role in a home that was handsome and practical and livable." Bill Gates, from *Bill Gates Speaks*, 1998.

BILL GATES

THE ROAD AHEAD

COMPANION INTERACTIVE CD-ROM INSIDE

This is the front cover of Gates's book, published in 1995. It will be interesting to see how many of his predictions for the future are correct.

Getting a Life

It was not long after their marriage in 1994 that children came along. Jennifer was born in 1996 and Rory in 1999. Fatherhood has genuinely changed Gates. Now if he is up all night, it is because he is caring for a crying baby, not looking for bugs on a computer program.

Gates's idea of relaxation is different from most other people's—he prefers to work long hours and doesn't need to switch off like most people do. This must be the secret of his greatness. Now Gates puts in only 12 hours a day at the office during the week and only 8 hours a day on the weekends! Somehow he still finds time to read. His favorite works include the American novels *The Great Gatsby* and *Catcher in the Rye*.

Bill and Melinda Gates arrive at the Seattle Cinerama in April 1999. She is seven months pregnant with their second child.

Gates gestures a lot when he is talking about something he thinks is important. Here he is defending the case of Microsoft at the White House Conference in April 2000.

He has always enjoyed fast cars. He usually drives a Porsche but also owns several Ferraris, a Lexus, and a Jaguar XJ6. As a young man he often got speeding tickets. One of his favorite ways of letting off steam was to drive fast at night in the desert around Albuquerque. These days he prefers quieter activities. He likes to relax over a game of bridge with Warren Buffett, the world's second richest man, or a round of golf with former U.S. President Bill Clinton.

"Time is the scarce resource and I treat it that way."
Bill Gates, *Bill Gates* by Lesinski.

Gates's best score at golf is 87. His ambition is to score 72 but he does not think he will achieve that.

Getting It Wrong

You don't become one of the richest people in the world by making lots of mistakes. This is certainly true of Bill Gates. He does make errors sometimes but he is very quick to spot them. He also has the ability to learn from his mistakes.

Probably his biggest mistake was failing to see the importance of the Internet. Initially, Gates thought the Internet would not take off. Fortunately for him, he was persuaded to change his mind in 1994 by some of the younger employees at Microsoft. Within a year Microsoft launched Internet Browser as part of the Windows 95 package.

> **"The closest thing to it (the Internet) I can think of is the Gold Rush where everybody went off to find their fortune."**
> Bill Gates in a speech at Learn Education Conference, Seattle, June 30, 1997.

Microsoft teamed up with Cisco Systems to produce new technology for using the Internet. Here Gates demonstrates an "Internet telephone."

Not everybody approves of Gates and his ways of doing business. This protest took place on the Microsoft campus in February 2000.

It was also possibly a mistake to make so many enemies, and to allow Microsoft to grow so big. The U.S. government did not like one company becoming so powerful, with such a large share (about 95 percent) of the computer software market. In 1998, Microsoft was taken to court by the Justice Department for illegal business practices. In June 2000, the judge ruled that Microsoft should be split up into two smaller businesses. Gates has appealed the decision.

In October 2000, Microsoft was in the news again when hackers managed to break in and copy secret codes for the software. Microsoft's reputation for security was badly damaged.

Distributing the Fortune

Gates's money is nearly all in Microsoft stock. Because the value of the stock changes from day to day, it is difficult to say exactly what he is worth. But on the "unofficial" Bill Gates website is a "wealth clock" showing how much money Bill Gates has at any given moment. On February 13, 2001 he was worth $67 billion.

In December 1998 the Gateses announced they were giving $100 million to establish a Children's Vaccine Program for developing countries.

In 1999, Gates set up the Bill and Melinda Gates Foundation, currently worth $21 billion. It is the largest charitable trust in the world. Its aim is to support projects connected with world health and education. The Foundation has recently given $26 million to research a cure for malaria, a disease that kills millions of people in poor countries.

This is what makes it all worth while! Gates smiles with satisfaction as children at Rumah Faith Orphanage in Malaysia show him their homepages.

Another $200 million has gone to Cambridge University in England to help students study science and technology.

Gates aims to be the biggest single benefactor in history. He was deeply moved on a visit to Africa where he saw desperately poor children without enough food to eat. It made him realize that computers were not the answer to the problems of poverty and disease. It was a turning point in his life.

> *"Mothers are going to walk right up to that computer and say to it, 'My children are dying—what can you do about it?'."*
> Gates speaking at a conference in Seattle in October 2000 on how computers are unable to help some people in the developing world.

The Shape of Things to Come

According to Gates, we are at the start of the Information Highway. It is difficult to imagine, but the Internet will soon be replaced by a far more powerful computer network called The Grid.

The Grid will be more secure and more reliable than the Internet. It will not be possible to infect it with viruses. Hackers will not be able to access secret information (as they did at Microsoft in October 2000). It will also be much, much bigger, rather like a 10-lane motorway compared with a country lane. Instead of going to the doctor, you will get a diagnosis and prescription via the screen and printer. People will pay for goods with a wallet-sized PC carried in a pocket. Everything will be digital.

Left: *Nelson Mandela, South Africa's first black President, made a big impression on Gates when they met at a Global Health Forum in Seattle in 1999. He admires the way Mandela thinks about politics and life.*

Right: *An electronic housedog is an example of what homes might contain in the future.*

Gates watches as one of his employees shows him a new video game console. The graphics are as realistic as a high-quality photograph.

As for Gates himself, he is still bubbling away with enthusiasm for the future. In June 2000, his company revealed their plans for Microsoft.NET. This will allow people to use the Internet with Microsoft software much more easily. But from time to time Gates has talked about retirement. So if anyone would like a top job in computing, there may be one sometime soon at Microsoft!

"Picking that next person (to become head of Microsoft) is something I give a lot of thought to. But it's probably five years before I have to do something very concrete about it."
Bill Gates, *The Times*, July 8, 1998.

45

Glossary

Access To be allowed entry into something.

Autistic A mental condition where the person has difficulty communicating.

Charitable Not profit-making.

Complex Difficult to understand.

Cornered the market Taken all the sales.

Diagnosis A doctor's decision about the kind of illness or disease a person has.

Digital Operated by pressing buttons which represent certain information codes within the computer.

Gifted Extremely talented or intelligent.

Hacker Somebody who uses their skill with computers to gain illegal access to computer networks.

Hardware The mechanical and electronic parts of a computer.

Illegal Against the law.

Infect To spread disease.

Internet The international computer network, or World-Wide Web, which offers links between businesses, schools and individuals.

Internet browser A computer program which allows users access to the Internet.

Investigate Look into something.

Irregular Without a fixed pattern.

Laid-back Not aggressive, calm.

Leasing agreement A legal arrangement where a person pays to borrow a product for a given time.

License Permission to use a product for a particular purpose.

Marquees Large tents used for special occasions.

Mathematical formulas Sets of numbers used to define ideas in maths.

Memorized Learned by heart.

Outclassed Beaten soundly by a competitor.

Pavilion A separate building.

Piracy Making an illegal copy of something, such as software.

Poker A game of cards.

Prescription A piece of paper from the doctor telling the chemist what medicines to give you.

Prosperous Wealthy, having plenty of money.

Respectable Having a good position in society.

Ruthless Without mercy, very determined.

Sarcastic Making fun of someone.

Self-made man Someone who made a lot of money after starting with nothing.

Software The programs and operating information used by a computer.

Specialized Adapted for a particular use.

Sued Being made to go to court and threatened with having to pay out large sums of money.

University campus The grounds around a college or university.

Virus A computer program that is designed to destroy computer systems or computer data.

Date Chart

1955 Bill Gates born, Seattle, Washington.

1967 Gates starts at Lakeside School. Meets Paul Allen. Forms club called the Lakeside Programmers.

1971 Signs first business deal with C-Cubed.

1973 Graduates from Lakeside and enrolls at Harvard University.

1974 Allen sees Altair 8800 advertised in *Popular Electronics*.

1975 Allen and Gates sell first software program for a microcomputer. Allen is offered job with MITS. Gates and Allen form Micro-Soft. Gates leaves Harvard to concentrate on new business.

1977 Micro-Soft breaks away from MITS.

1979 Microsoft loses hyphen and moves to Seattle.

1980 IBM asks Microsoft to write software program for new PC.

1982 Allen resigns because of ill health.

1983 Microsoft launches Word program with color pictures for choices and mouse to click and point.

1986 Microsoft is floated on New York Stock Exchange.

1987 Gates becomes world's youngest-ever billionaire at 32-years-old.

1989 Partnership with IBM breaks down.

1990 Windows 3.0 is launched.

1992 Windows 3.1 is launched.

1994 Marries Melinda French. Gates's mother dies from breast cancer.

1995 Launch of Windows 95. Becomes world's richest man, worth $12.9 billion. Publishes bestseller *The Road Ahead*.

1996 First child, Jennifer, is born.

1998 Sued by Justice Department.

1999 Second child, Rory, is born. Sets up Bill and Melinda Gates Foundation.

2000 Microsoft loses court action brought by Justice Department. Plans for Microsoft.NET are launched. Hackers break into Microsoft.

Further Information

Books for Younger Readers

Connolly, Sean. *Bill Gates*. Des Plaines, IL: Heinemann, 1999.

Simon, Charnan. *Bill Gates: Helping People Use Computers (Community Builders)*. Danbury, CT: Children's Press, 1998.

Books for Older Readers/Sources

Dickinson, Joan D. *Bill Gates: Billionaire Computer Genius (People to Know)*. Berkeley Heights, NJ: Enslow Publishers, 1997.

Lesinski, Jeanne D. *Bill Gates*. Minneapolis: Lerner Publishing Group, 2000.

Website addresses

http://www.microsoft.com/billgates/default.asp
Microsoft's official pages on Gates.

http://www.glf.org
Bill and Melinda Gates Foundation.

Index

Page numbers in **bold** mean there is a picture on the page.